Berklee

In the Pocket

Ultimate DJ

Stephen Webber

Berklee Media

Vice President: Dave Kusek
Dean of Continuing Education: Debbie Cavalier
Director of Business Affairs: Rob Green
Technology Manager: Mike Serio
Marketing Manager, Berkleemusic: Barry Kelly
Senior Graphic Designer: David Ehlers

Berklee Press

Senior Writer/Editor: Jonathan Feist
Writer/Editor: Susan Gedutis Lindsay
Production Manager: Shawn Girsberger
Marketing Manager, Berklee Press: Jennifer Rassler
Product Marketing Manager: David Goldberg

ISBN 0-87639-055-6

berklee press

DISTRIBUTED BY
LEONARD®
ORATION
UND RD. P.O. BOX 13819
WISCONSIN 53213

1140 Boylston
Boston, MA 02
(617) 747-2146

Visit Berklee

www.berkle

eonard Online at
lleonard.com

Printed in the United States of America by Patterson Printing
11 10 09 08 07 06 05 04   5 4 3 2 1

Contents

1. Introduction

You can take the study of DJing and playing the turn-table as far as your imagination, discipline, and desire lead you.

Fig. 1.1. Playing the turntable

This book is meant to serve as a quick-start for setting up, and learning the basics of cueing, beat matching, and scratching.

What Kind of Instrument Is This, Anyway?

Okay, we all know that you can use a turntable to play records, and that can be a pretty great thing all by itself (depending on your record collection).

In addition, the turntable can be approached as a musical instrument of amazing depth and versatility. It is very effective as a percussion instrument, capable of producing precise and complex rhythmic figures for solos, or inventive fills between vocal and instrumental lines.

Combined with a mixer, a turntable can also be used as an analog sampler. It can play spoken words and musical phrases, forward or backward, at any speed, pitch, or volume.

With two turntables, you can morph beats into different time signatures and tempos on the spot. You can cut and paste sounds seamlessly in real time, in front of an audience.

The turntable/mixer setup is also similar to a synthesizer. You can control the attack, decay, sustain, and release (ADSR) of any tone in real time using the mixer's faders.

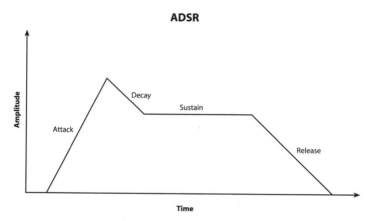

Fig. 1.2. ADSR synthesis chart

The turntable can be a melodic instrument, too. Using records with sustained tones, you can play melodies by manipulating the pitch slider and the 33-1/3 and 45 speed buttons. You can glide in and out of notes, and achieve musical effects such as vibrato and tremolo.

Like a synthesizer or sampler, the turntable can be transformed into thousands of different instruments, just by changing records. But unlike many digital machines, playing the turntable is a physical experience, more like pulling a bow across a cello string than pushing a button or clicking a mouse.

If using the turntable as a musical instrument still seems farfetched, consider that the bow itself started out as a weapon for prehistoric humans, and developed into a sophisticated device for making music. It seems less of a leap to consider that the turntable (a device invented to play music) could evolve into an expressive instrument.

Continued innovations, such as more extensive pitch controls, will help the turntable reach its full potential. But the turntable has already been adapted by imaginative musicians to create new musical forms capable of conveying emotion from one human being to another. And that is the true test of any instrument.

Beyond the Turntable...

The ability of a DJ to captivate a dance floor with their knowledge of records, musicianship, and ability to read the crowd are also crucial aspects of the DJ tradition.

For a more complete method on playing the turntable, pick up *Turntable Technique* (book/2-Record Set) from Berklee Press. The book includes play-along exercises, and interviews with many top DJs, including QBert, Craze, Swamp, A-Trak, and MixMaster Mike.

2. Equipment

The Basic Setup

The basic turntable DJ setup is made up of:

- two turntables (with cartridges and slip mats)
- a DJ mixer

You'll need an amplified stereo playback system to hear what you're doing. Headphones will come in handy for cueing up records.

Just add records and mix....

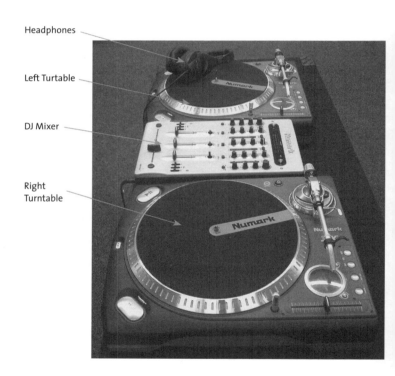

Headphones

Left Turtable

DJ Mixer

Right
Turntable

FIG. 2.1. A basic turntable DJ setup

It's important that you set up your equipment on a very sturdy surface. You don't want your equipment to shift from side to side while you are scratching.

Set up your turntables and mixer at the same height. A little above the waist seems the preferred level for most DJs. Experiment to find the most comfortable height for you.

Turntables

There are many excellent turntables on the market today. The high-end models tend to be heavy, precision instruments that absorb shock and avoid skips.

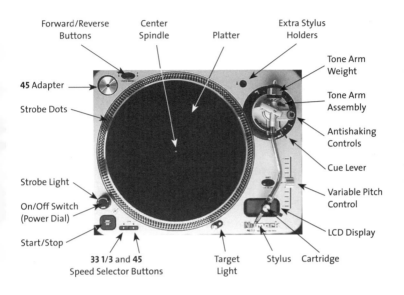

FIG. 2.2. Turntable

With few variations, DJ turntables all have the following components:

On/Off Switch (Power Dial) Provides power to the turntable's stylus, but does not spin the platter. There are scratching techniques, such as the "basic (or baby) scratch," that will take advantage of this separation.

Start/Stop Button Engages or disengages the turntable's motor, causing the platter to spin or to stop spinning. Pressing this button while the record is playing gives a "grinding to a halt" effect, which can be put to good use. There are modifications that allow the turntable to spin backwards by double clicking on this control. The turntable pictured features separate forward/reverse buttons.

33-1/3 and 45 Speed Selector Buttons Control the speed the platter spins, measured in "revolutions per minute" (rpm). At 33-1/3 rpm, a record completes 33 and 1/3 rotations in one minute.

Variable Pitch Control Changes the speed of a record, which also changes the pitch. Most DJ turntables have a single sliding Variable Pitch control for both 33-1/3 rpm and 45 rpm settings. Some have two sliders: one for 33-1/3 rpm and another for 45 rpm.

These controls come in handy while beat matching. By altering the speed of a new record (while listening in the headphones), you can match the tempo of the record that is already playing on the other turntable.

Variable pitch controls and 33/45 switches can also be used to play melodies by playing a record of a constant tone.

Cue Lever   Lifts and lowers the tone arm. Not many professional DJs use the cue lever all that much. I recommend that you get comfortable lifting the tone arm by hand and placing it accurately on the record.

Cartridge   Houses the stylus. Many cartridges mount into the head-shell assembly with two screws. Four color-coded wires connect to terminals of the same color. When you install a cartridge, be sure to follow the installation instructions carefully. There are several sturdy cartridges available for scratch DJs. Some come with their own head-shell assembly. The head-shell assembly mounts in the tone-arm tube lock and is held in place by turning the lock ring clockwise (when viewed from the rear).

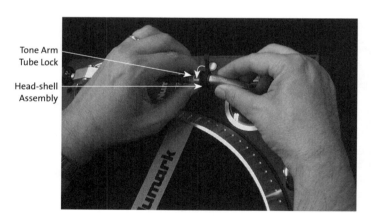

FIG. 2.3. Mounting the head-shell assembly

Stylus   Includes the needle, which makes direct contact with the records. The stylus mounts onto the cartridge. A new stylus usually ships with a needle protector; you'll obviously need to remove this before playing records. How often you replace your stylus depends on wear. Contributing factors include the amount of weight you use, your individual scratching style, and how well everything is aligned. *Tip:* Always take an extra stylus or two with you to a gig. While most of the time a stylus wears down slowly, it is possible for the tip to break suddenly.

Tone Arm Supports the stylus and carries the connections (wires) from the stylus to the turntable. At the back end of the tone arm are the weights; at the front end, the cartridge. Many DJs set up the turntable so that the tone arm is across the top, out of the way.

Tone-Arm Weight Regulates the pressure on the stylus. Generally, the more weight on the tone arm, the more pressure on the needle to stay in the grooves, which can minimize skipping. However, more weight can wear out records faster and cause "burning" (saturating records with white noise). Another possible downside to more weight is increased needle wear.

FIG. 2.4. Adjusting the tone-arm weight

To increase the amount of weight on the tone arm, rotate the weight so that it moves towards the stylus end of the tone arm.

FIG. 2.5. The tone-arm weight mounted backwards

Tip: If you put the tone-arm weight on backwards, this moves more weight forward, increasing the weight bearing down on the stylus.

Tone-Arm Height Adjustment Changes the angle of the stylus in the groove. Some DJs prefer to raise the tone arm to angle the stylus down in the groove. To adjust the height of the tone arm on many DJ turntables, grip the base of the tone-arm assembly and turn it.

Fig. 2.6. Adjusting the tone-arm height

How you set up your tone arm depends on a few things, such as the cartridge and stylus you're using, your touch, and your individual style. DJ QBert likes to adjust the tone arm so the top of the cartridge is just above the surface of the record.

If any part of the stylus or cartridge other than the needle has contact with the record, your tone-arm height and weight adjustments aren't right, and things are going to skip.

Antiskating Control Helps keep the needle from skipping, or skating, out of the record grooves. Most manuals advise setting the antiskating control to the same numeric setting as the tone-arm weight. If you increase the tone-arm weight by turning it around, try setting the antiskating control as high as it will go. Again, experiment to see what works best for you.

Dust Cover/Hinges You'll want to remove the dust cover entirely before mixing. You can lift the dust cover out of its hinges by opening it first, then lifting it straight up. It's a good idea to put the dust cover on while transporting your turntable.

DJ Mixers

Inputs and Outputs The typical DJ mixer has stereo inputs for two turntables and a microphone, and outputs for stereo headphones and for feeding either a home stereo, PA system, or recording console. Some mixers have extra stereo inputs for other sources, such as tape machines or CD players. More advanced mixers have additional outputs and inputs (known as "sends" and "returns") for hooking up external effects devices.

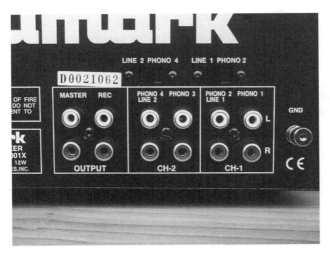

FIG. 2.7. Inputs and outputs for a basic DJ mixer

A turntable connection consists of two RCA connectors (left and right channels) and a ground wire connection. It's important to connect and hold the ground wire in place around the ground post by tightening the thumbscrew. If you don't connect the ground wire to the ground post, you'll get massive hum or buzz noises in your system. *Tip:* You can't plug a turntable directly into a tape recorder or mixing board without going through a phono preamp first. The phono preamp boosts the output signal of the turntable cartridge. DJ mixers have these preamps built in, as do home stereo amplifiers/receivers.

Controls The three controls used most often are the crossfader (for mixing the two turntables together), the up-faders or "volume faders," and the on/off switches on each turntable.

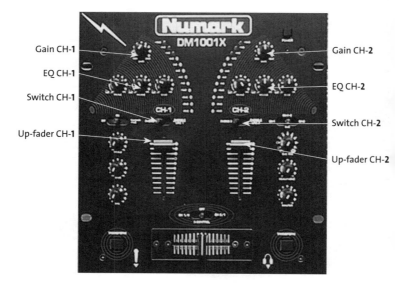

FIG. 2.8. Controls on a DJ mixer

Additional controls include gain controls, to adjust the phono preamps for each turntable; cue sends, to route each turntable's signal to the headphones; and a head-phone volume control.

Many DJ mixers include equalization or EQ controls for each turntable. EQ controls let you shape the sound by adjusting the bass, midrange, and treble frequencies.

The most powerful EQ sections on DJ mixers can kill entire frequency ranges, giving you increased flexibility in creating arrangements.

Other bells and whistles on professional DJ mixers include built-in effects, automatic tempo sensing, and adjustable crossfader curves.

Playback Systems You'll need to plug the outputs of your DJ mixer into an amplifier and speakers to hear what you're doing. On your DJ mixer, put the crossfader to the middle, set the channel switches to "phono" or "on," and put the up-faders about halfway up. Keep the gain pots low at first, say a quarter of the way up.

Home Stereo Plug into the "aux input" of your boom box or home stereo system's receiver/amplifier with two male-to-male RCA cables. Connect the other end to the output of your DJ mixer, which will be labeled "amplifier output" or something similar.

Make sure that the aux input is selected on your stereo system, and start with the volume all the way down. Play a record on one of your turntables, while slowly turning up the volume of your stereo system to a moderately low level. You should hear the record playing.

If you don't, check all of your controls and connections while keeping the volume on your stereo LOW! Chances are that you'll fix the problem by flipping a channel switch or something similar, and if you've jacked up the volume you could do serious damage to your speakers.

PA System   The quality, size, and power of your PA system will be one of the determining factors in what kind of gigs you can handle.

Most professional DJ mixers provide low impedance (Low Z) outputs, often with 1/4" TRS (Tip Ring Sleeve) connections. You can plug these outputs directly into a professional amplifier's inputs, which are usually 1/4" jacks or three-pronged (XLR) connectors.

From the amplifier, the signal must be sent to speakers, usually through speaker cables with 1/4" ends or "banana plugs." If all of your cables have 1/4" ends, it's important to realize that there is a difference between speaker cables and the cables that go between your mixer and amplifier. It is a good idea to label all of your cables.

If you're playing at a large club, chances are there will be a house PA system. Many visiting DJs will bring in their own cartridges, and use the house turntables and mixer. If the club's setup is significantly different than your own, you may decide to use your own mixer and turntables. You should work this out with the club's management (and/or house DJ) before the gig.

If you are playing turntables in a band, you'll need to interface with the band's PA system. A few PA mixers have high impedance stereo inputs on RCA jacks, which are okay to use if you're very close (less than 10 feet) to the inputs. You're better off using 1/4" or XLR channel inputs. If your mixer only has RCA jacks, you may need to buy adapters or transformers.

Figure out what cables and adapters you'll need to connect to the PA you'll be working with well before the gig, and be sure to carry a few extra cables with you just in case.

Tape Recorder Tip

Many DJ mixers let you plug into a tape recorder at the same time. Most tape decks accept either RCA or 1/4" inputs. Follow the instructions that came with your recording device to set your input levels.

Volume Tip

Experts tell us that what contributes most to hearing loss is exposure to high levels of volume for long periods of time. Keep your volume at reasonable levels. Carry earplugs with you when you go to concerts where you're not in charge of the volume level. I know many musicians who have suffered permanent hearing loss from their own constant playing of loud music, and not one of them thinks it was worth it.

Setting Up

In standard mode (figure 2.9), the tone arms are accessible near the front of the turntable. This works fine for cueing and playing records.

FIG. 2.9. Standard mode

Most turntablists and scratch DJs set up their turntables with the tone arm across the top rather than on the side. This is commonly referred to as battle mode (figure 2.10).

FIG. 2.10. Battle mode

In battle mode, the tone arms are up and out of the way. This is more suited to scratching, beat juggling, and other techniques. There are at least a dozen less common variations on these two setups, like the "duck rock mode," and the "left-handed lateral mode." While the majority of DJs starting out today gravitate towards the battle mode, you can execute the techniques in this book using any of the modes mentioned.

Slip Mats

Slip mats are twelve-inch discs that go between the turntable's platter and the record. When you are scratching, cueing, or otherwise holding back the record while the turntable's platter is spinning, the slip mat serves as a buffer.

FIG. 2.11. Slip mat

If your turntable came with a rubber mat to put on the platter (most do), don't use it. It will make scratching much more difficult. You most likely received one or two slip mats along with your DJ equipment. If not, they are inexpensive (a few bucks at the most) and available wherever DJ gear is sold.

Slip mats allow the turntable to spin while you manipulate the record. When you let go of the record, the slip mat and the record use gravity and friction to reconnect with the turntable's spinning platter and return to speed.

At first, it may seem hard to manipulate your records while the platter is spinning. The more you work with a particular record, the easier it will be to manipulate. This is known as "breaking in" a record.

Custom Plastic Slip Mats

An additional slip mat, made of clear plastic, is a tool that many turntablists find helpful. If you're having a hard time manipulating your records independently of the turntable's platter, this could help considerably.

FIG. 2.12. Plastic slip mat

For step-by-step instructions on making your own plastic slip mat, check out the *Turntable Technique* method from Berklee Press.

3. Preparing to Play

Which Hand Does What?

For most instruments, the formula is set. Take the guitar, for example. For right-handed players, the left hand is always on the guitar neck, while the right hand generates the sound by strumming, picking, or plucking the strings. Most lefties (like Jimi Hendrix and Paul McCartney) flip the guitar over and string it upside-down so their dominant hand still sets the strings in motion.

Unlike the guitar, a pair of turntables set up in battle mode is a symmetrical setup. Both hands have equal access to the records and the mixer.

When first starting to play turntables, many DJs use their dominant hand to manipulate the records, because that's where it seems all the action is. However, after playing for awhile, most realize how important the mixing hand is.

These days, scratch DJs do things with the crossfader that are just as intricate as what they do with the records. The fader hand plays sixteenth notes and triplets with lightning-fast techniques, such as the "crab" and the "transformer."

Fig. 3.1. Intricate fader technique often attracts the DJ's dominant hand.

Once you start practicing these techniques, you may find it easier to use your nondominant hand to manipulate the record you're scratching and your dominant hand for the fast fader moves.

At first, it may take all the coordination you have to get the records to behave the way you want. Eventually, though, the demands of the fader become more obvious.

Be Ambidextrous

It's important to develop the ability to manipulate the turntable and the DJ mixer with either hand. While your dominant hand may gravitate to the more difficult task, there are many situations where it pays to be a "switch hitter," as they say in baseball—able to use either hand. Beat juggling, sitting in with another DJ and sharing two turntables, and playing in a turntable ensemble are a few examples.

Fig. 3.2. Ambidextrous technique

Spend time practicing each technique with both hands. It will pay off.

4. Cueing Records

Cueing means finding the exact spot on a record to play. This could be the downbeat of track 1, the drum break of track 3, or the sound effect halfway into track 4 on side 2.

The tracks on a record are numbered from the outside moving in. The silent spaces between tracks show up as smooth areas that separate the tracks from each other.

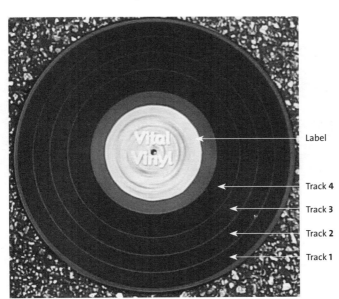

Label

Track **4**

Track **3**

Track **2**

Track **1**

FIG 4.1. Record with tracks labeled

Using the Start/Stop Button

Back when vinyl records were played on the radio, DJs would cue them up and then set them in motion using the start/stop button. It's the easiest way to start getting the hang of it.

Make sure your hands are clean (you don't want to get dirt all over your records!) and your playback system is on. On the mixer, turn the turntable's volume fader up and the crossfader to the center. Place a record on top of a slip mat on the turntable platter. Press the start/stop button on your turntable to start the platter spinning.

1. Carefully place the stylus at the beginning of the record.

2. As soon as you hear the first sound, press the start/stop button to stop the record from turning. You should hear the record quickly grind to a halt.

3. Ease your middle finger onto the record in the smooth space between the label and the end of the last track.

4. Rotate the record backwards (counterclockwise), until the stylus is at the beginning of the track. This is called backspinning. You should hear what's on the record (in this case, the count-off) going backwards.

FIG. 4.2. Backspinning

5. Rotate the record forward (clockwise) until you hear the first sound on the record.

6. Rock the record back and forth until you locate the exact beginning of the track.

7. Back the record up slightly to give the turntable space to get up to speed. You're now ready to play the track.

8. Press the start/stop button to play the track.

Listen carefully to make sure that the record is up to speed by the time the audio begins. If you hear the pitch sliding up as the track begins, back up more in step 7. If there is too much time before the record starts, back up less in step 7.

Repeat these steps until you get the hang of it. With practice, you'll get to know exactly how much space your turntable needs to get up to speed.

On the Fly

You can also set the starting place for a record by hand while the platter is spinning. This allows you to cue things up quickly, on the fly. With the platter already spinning, the record can get back up to speed faster. Here's how:

1. Place the stylus at the beginning of the already-spinning record.

2. As soon as you hear the first sound on the record, gently rest your middle finger on the smooth area between the label and the last track.

3. Apply just enough pressure to drag the record to a stop while the platter continues to turn underneath.

4. Backspin the record to the start of the track.

5. Rotate the record forward again (clockwise) until you hear the first sound on the record. You may want to rock the record back and forth until you locate the exact beginning of the track, applying slight pressure to the body of the record.

6. Set the record in motion in such a way that it instantly returns to playing speed. Rather than lifting your hand straight up, release the record by moving your finger tips slightly in a forward direction.

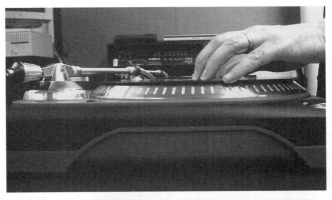

(A)

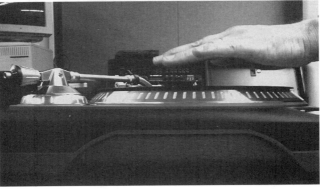

(B)

FIG. 4.3. (A) Grasping the body of the record, and (B) releasing the record

If you hear the record sliding up to speed, work on your release. Make sure you're not pushing down too hard and slowing the platter. If the record seems too fast for the first moment of playback, back off on your forward nudge.

Practice cueing by hand until the technique becomes second nature. This could take dozens of spins, so be patient!

Cueing in Time

"In time" means that you are right in sync with the tempo of whatever you're playing along with. As you move on to mixing, blending, and beat matching, it's important that you can start a record in time. The following proce- dure can help you develop this skill:

1. Play enough of the track you're working with to get a feel for the tempo.

2. Tap your foot or nod your head in time with the beat as you backspin and cue the record.

3. Now, count the record down in time with the track, "One! Two! Three! Four!" rocking the record back and forth slightly with each beat.

4. Set the record in motion an instant before the next beat, so that the record starts perfectly in time with your countdown.

Repeat these steps until you can nail it every time.

FIG. 4.4. Setting the record in motion

Marking Records

Marking records helps you visualize the beginning of a track. This is incredibly helpful when beat matching, beat juggling, or even just cueing records. Often, having a record marked can reduce or even negate the need for headphones.

Most DJs mark their record with an adhesive label or tape. Cassette labels and adhesive dots are two favorites. You can buy adhesive dots at office and educational supply stores. Never use tape that has gummy adhesive (like masking tape, duct tape, or packing tape).

To mark the beginning of track 1, first locate the exact beginning of the track. (Follow the steps in "Cueing Using the Start/Stop Button.") When you locate the exact beginning of the track, put your marker on the outer edge of the label.

FIG. 4.5. Marking a record using adhesive dots

There is no real standard place to mark a record. Some DJs will put the dot or cassette label at 12 o'clock, others will have it point to the stylus illumination light, the stylus itself, or even the on/off switch.

My advice is to experiment. Place your mark somewhere, try cueing the record a few times, then move the mark somewhere else and try cueing some more. Leave your mark wherever it works best for your particular hand-eye coordination.

You can also mark the location of a specific word, sound effect, or other audio event by placing a piece of tape on the track itself, right next to the targeted sound. Use a smaller piece of tape, and make sure the corners are pressed down securely so the tape won't come into contact with the head shell as it passes over. Start by placing the tape exactly one groove out from the targeted sound, but experiment to see what works best in each situation.

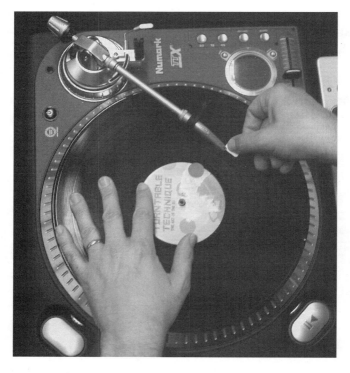

FIG. 4.6. Marking the exact location of a sound

5. Beat Matching

Beat matching means getting two records perfectly in sync with each other. You can then use the crossfader to switch between them. Beat matching is a skill that every DJ must master. When you're playing a rave, party, dance, or club, being able to segue (pronounced *seg-way*, meaning, to transition smoothly) from one record to another without losing the beat will help you keep the dance floor full. Beat matching must be second nature if you are going to get into beat juggling, a main component of many scratch-mixing routines.

You can beat match any two records that are close to the same tempo and have complementary beats by adjusting the variable pitch controls on each turntable. It's a good idea to write down the tempos of the different tracks in your collection on the record label or sleeve, or on a list you keep with your records.

Tempos are expressed in beats per minute (bpm). There are devices that can help you find the bpm of any song. For instance, the "Dr. Beat" metronome by Boss lets you tap along with the beat to find the tempo. "Dr. Beat" displays the bpm numerically after four taps. There are more sophisticated devices, like the Numark "Beatkeeper II," that detect bpm automatically; a few DJ mixers even have them built in. *Tip:* Another key concept is that beats come in groups (usually of four), known as "bars" or "measures." When you're beat matching, it's important to have a good feel for where these bars begin and end.

In most hip-hop, rock, and funk styles, the first beat of each bar is usually played by the "kick" drum (also known as the "bass" drum), which often has a deep, low tone. The "snare" drum, usually higher in pitch, often plays on the second (and/or fourth) beats.

If you are new to this, practice counting beats until it becomes easy. Listen to a groove, identify the first beat (also known as the "downbeat") of each bar, and then try counting along: "One, two, three, four." As you begin your excursions into beat matching, try to keep your bars lined up.

Begin by cueing up two copies of the same record (follow the steps in the section, "Cueing Using the Start/Stop Buttons.") When you've got the records cued up and ready to play:

1. Start the record on your right and let it play.

2. Get yourself in sync with the beat. (Tap your foot or nod your head, and count the beats!)

3. With the index, middle, and ring fingers of your left hand, press down on the left record. Use your thumb to press the start/stop button.

FIG. 5.1. Starting the platter while holding the record

4. Let the platter spin up to speed while you keep the record from moving.

5. Count down four beats, then spin the record you're holding at just the right moment to synchronize the downbeats on the two records.

If you miss, you can just let the record on your right keep playing, backspin the record on your left to the top, and try setting it in motion again. You may have to try this several times before you get the two records in perfect sync.

Let's say you've gotten both records going and you're close to being perfectly in sync, but not quite. Rather than stopping one of the records, you can use one of the following techniques:

Spinning the Label

1. Decide which record is behind. (The headphones can be helpful for this.)

2. Place your middle finger on the label of the record that's behind, spinning your finger along with the record.

3. Let your finger spin a little faster, pushing the record along with it.

4. Listen closely to determine when you have gotten the two records in sync—or if you're getting farther apart!

FIG. 5.2. Spinning the label

Dragging the Platter

1. Determine which record is ahead.

2. Drag your middle finger against the side of the platter that the record is on, slowing down the record slightly.

3. Listen closely to determine when the two records are in sync—or whether they're getting farther apart!

FIG. 5.3. Dragging the platter

Get on in there and spin. Drag up a storm until you've gotten the hang of it. Once you get comfortable with these techniques, beat matching becomes a breeze.

You may need to use the variable pitch control on your turntables to perfectly match beats on two records. If you are matching beats on two different songs, you will almost always need the variable pitch control. Some DJs get two records in sync using only the variable pitch control, speeding up and slowing down the record without spinning the label or dragging the platter.

When two copies of the same record are close to being in sync, the records will sound "phased." Or, if the records are already in sync, when they start to sound phased, it's a sign that they are drifting apart. You can also use this sound, also referred to as "flanging," as a musical effect.

Cueing with Headphones

When you're mixing for an audience, you'll probably want to be able to cue a record without the audience hearing it. This is where headphone cueing comes in.

Suppose you want to get the next record ready to play on the left turntable while your audience is hearing the record playing on the right turntable.

1. Make sure the crossfader is all the way over to the right.

2. Set the mixer's cue switch to monitor the left turntable (often labeled CH-1 or Program-1) in your headphones.

3. Listening through your headphones, cue up the record on the left turntable. (Follow the steps in the previous sections.)

4. Make sure the volume fader is up for the left turntable (CH-1 or Program-1).

5. When you're ready for the audience to hear the next record, use the crossfader to segue between the two records.

Fig. 5.4. Cueing with headphones, one ear off

Tips:

- If you are matching the beat of the record in your headphones to a record that's playing over the sound system, slide one ear out of the headphones as you cue it up, so you can hear both records. There are headphones made just for DJs that have only one earpiece.

- Practice cueing with headphones for both the right and left turntables.

Creative Mixing

How you put together and mix a set is a big part of what defines your style.

Edan, a talented Boston DJ and MC, suggests, "Look for tracks that complement each other, and mix them in a way that pays tribute to the music."

Records containing "club mixes" often feature long, unstructured intros and outros that allow DJs to cross-fade in and out of records without matching beats.

When you do beat match two different songs, you can do some creative mixing by using the crossfader to go back and forth between the two.

To start getting the hang of this, beat match two different tracks that share the same tempo.

Mix the tracks together for awhile, then crossfade back and forth between the two, making sure that the sync between the two remains solid. Try slamming the crossfader back and forth every eight bars, every four bars, every two bars, every bar, every two beats, every beat, and every half beat! Be creative and create your own arrangement.

You can also use more advanced crossfader techniques such as the "crab" and the "transformer" (taught in *Turntable Technique*) when mixing beats.

Search your record collection for other songs and tracks to play together. Remember, the variable pitch control on your turntables can help match tempos between songs where the tempos aren't the same.

Build up your record collection, and develop your own style, your own taste. Most of all, enjoy yourself!

6. The Basic Scratch

The basic scratch is also known as the "baby scratch." For the basic scratch, you only manipulate the record, not the fader. You can scratch virtually any sound, with a wide variety of results.

It's helpful to begin using a track with a long sustained sound, in case the needle skips to a different part of the track. If you can, use a record that has a track with constant white noise, like *Turntable Technique*.

On the mixer, put the volume fader up and the crossfader to the center.

Playing the Basic Scratch

1. Place the record on top of a slip mat on the turntable's platter.

2. Press the start/stop button to start the platter spinning.

3. Carefully place the stylus at the beginning of the track.

4. Let the noise play for a few seconds.

5. Press the start/stop button again to stop the record.

6. Place the tips of your index, middle, and ring fingers on the record, and slowly drag the record back and forth. Keep your wrist relaxed and your motions fluid.

Congratulations, you're scratching! Experiment with scratching at different speeds. Improvise (make up) different rhythms.

Study the following pictures for correct hand position.

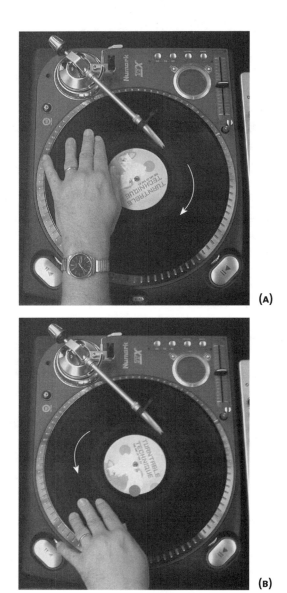

FIG. 6.1. (A) Basic scratch (forward), and **(B)** basic scratch (back)

The pitch of the scratch (how high or low it is) depends on two things: the pitch of the recorded track, and the speed that you are dragging the record. Notice the changing pitch of the sound as you alter the speed of your scratch.

The volume of the scratch also depends on two things: how high you set the faders on the mixer, and how fast you drag the record (the velocity of the scratch).

On lightweight, less expensive turntables, the tone arms may tend to bounce, skipping the needle to different sections of the track, or sometimes even to different tracks. Skipping can be a signal that you are pushing down too hard, bouncing the record.

To avoid skipping, lighten your touch. Turn the record with your fingers, moving it smoothly back and forth with only a slight, constant pressure. Let your fingers pivot. Remember, no bouncing!

TIPS:

- Practice on both turntables.

- Practice both hands.

- While improvising rhythms, remember that the silence between the notes is just as important as the notes themselves.

- Use a light touch to reduce skipping.

Adding a Beat

When you feel comfortable with the basic scratch, try adding a beat on the second turntable and playing along.

On the mixer, raise the volume faders for both turntables, and set the crossfader to the center. On your second turntable, cue up a track that has a medium-tempo groove and some musical space you can fill with scratch rhythms.

Be tasteful, and try phrasing your scratches like a melody or a conversation.

If you want to learn more about scratching, check out the exercises in the *Turntable Technique* method from Berklee Press. This method comes with records containing excellent scratch material, beats to match and scratch over, and all of the scratching exercises played to a beat. For even more help, check out the *Turntable Technique* DVD (also available on VHS).

7. Mixer Exercises

Playing the Up-Fader

The up-fader (or "volume fader") adds another dimension to playing the turntable. DJ mixers come with two or more up-faders to control the volume of each turntable. They can be labeled CH-1 and CH-2 for channels 1 and 2, and PGM 1 and PGM 2 for programs 1 and 2, or something similar.

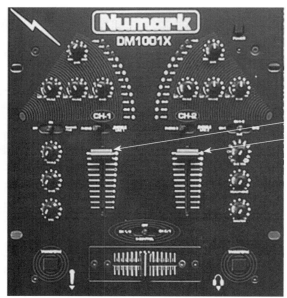

Up-fader CH-**1**
Up-fader CH-**2**

FIG. 7.1. Up-faders

First, let's get the hang of using the up-fader musically, in rhythm:

1. Cue up a continuous tone.

2. Adjust the mixer's gain controls and your playback system so the tone is at a decent level when the volume fader is set all the way up. It should be loud enough to function as a lead instrument, but not deafening.

3. Put the crossfader into the center.

4. Turn the channel's switch to the "on" or "phono" position.

5. Starting with the up-fader all the way down, use your thumb to push it up to the top in one quick, smooth motion.

6. Use your index finger to push the up-fader back down to zero in another quick, smooth motion.

You should hear the fader click as it hits the top and the bottom of its range.

Repeat steps 5 and 6 with both hands, keeping your wrist loose.

FIG. 7.2. (A) Up-fader up, and **(B)** up-fader down

See how fast you can thrust the up-fader up and down. Try leaving it up for different lengths of time, playing longer notes and shorter notes. Remember to keep your fingers, wrist, and arm relaxed.

Cue up and play a beat on your second turntable. Improvise some rhythms with the volume fader on the first turntable over the beats from the second turntable.

Try using continuous tones or sounds, or white noise, like a train or babbling brook.

Playing the Switch

Located at the top of the up-fader is the channel switch, also known as the "on/off switch," the "phono-line switch," or simply the "switch." To play the switch, make sure the up-fader is up and the crossfader is near the center.

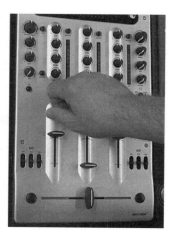

FIG. 7.3. Playing the switch

Play a constant tone. Practice turning the switch on and off to play notes of different lengths, just like you did with the up-fader. Have some fun improvising. Remember to keep your fingers, wrist, and arm relaxed. Try moving between the switch and the up-fader.

Use the Vari-Speed controls on your turntable to change the pitch of the tone, using the up-fader and switch to turn on and off the different notes. Use a low synth tone to build a bass line, or higher pitched tones to play melodies. The *Turntablist's Toolkit* is an excellent source of tones for just this purpose.

8. Combining Both Hands

So far, we've been working with the record and the fader separately, and with good reason. The old adage "divide and conquer" isn't just about strategy on the battlefield. Breaking a new skill down into individual parts is just as helpful in learning to play the turntable as it is in learning the martial arts, or playing the piano.

The following techniques will use both hands, combining fader moves and record manipulations. If you are having trouble with any of these techniques at first, try practicing each hand separately.

Also, be sure to review the exercises we've gone through so far. Use different sounds in your scratching, and find progressively faster break beats to work out over.

The Stab

The stab is a short and powerful burst of sound, executed by coordinating abrupt motions of both the fader and the record. Both hands must work together. To execute the stab:

1. Cue up a continuous noise or tone.

2. Start with the up-fader down all the way.

3. Hold the record still, letting the platter spin underneath.

4. Push the record away from you (executing a forward stroke) while simultaneously throwing the fader up.

5. Immediately pull the fader back down.

6. Pull the record back towards you (executing a back stroke) in silence.

Fig. 8.1. The stab

Steps 4 through 6 happen in one quick, violent motion, thus the name: "the stab." Note that both hands are moving in the same direction at the same time, making this one of the easier scratching techniques to coordinate.

The stab is most effective when you only hear the forward stroke. Make sure that you bring the fader down quickly to mute the sound of the back stroke.

If you have trouble keeping the platter spinning while you hold the record, you can also execute the stab with the platter at rest. However, you should work on getting the hang of letting the platter spin while you manipulate the record. Soon, you'll be combining the stab with other techniques that require a spinning platter.

Sometimes it's easier to get a grip closer to the label. Do this when you need to, but work on getting comfortable grabbing the record anywhere without slowing the platter. Check the illuminated dots on the side of the platter—if they appear stationary, then the platter is spinning up to speed.

You can also perform stabs using the switch instead of the fader. The switch gives you a sharper, more precise sound, because the signal comes on instantly at full power, rather than fading in and out.

Cutting

Cutting, also known as "forward," repeats a short sample of sound from a record, like a keyboardist uses a digital sampler. You can use any sound for cutting: a word, a phrase, a brass stab, a snare drum, a burst of noise, you name it!

The key to cutting is to keep track of exactly where the sound you're using begins on the record. Mark the location of the sample with an adhesive dot or cassette label. Visualize where your fingers need to catch the record in order to bring the sound back to the beginning.

To practice cutting, first choose a sound. We'll call this the "sample." On the mixer, put the crossfader in the middle.

1. With the platter spinning, cue up the sample, and hold the record just before the beginning of the sound.

FIG. 8.2. Holding the record

2. Set the record in motion, letting the sample play, fader up.

FIG. 8.3. Playing the sample

3. Catch the record at the spot you were just holding onto, and quickly bring the fader all the way down.

FIG. 8.4. Catching the sample

4. Bring the record back to the starting point with the fader down.

FIG. 8.5. Bringing the sample back

5. Repeat steps 2 through 4, firing at will.

Cutting is similar to the stab, except that when you cut, you let the turntable play the sound, rather than pushing it forward yourself. As with the stab, it's important to mute the entire back scrape to keep your cuts clean and tight sounding.

9. Using the Crossfader

First, let's look at how the crossfader works.

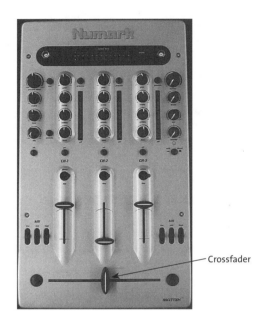

Crossfader

FIG. 9.1. Crossfader

Most crossfaders on DJ mixers weren't designed to provide an even crossfade between the two channels. There is usually a large space in the middle of the range (about half the length of the crossfader) where both turntables are up to full volume. Many of the more advanced DJ mixers let you adjust the curve of the crossfader to suit your taste.

Locating the Cut-On Point

The cut-on point is the point where the sound from the opposite channel suddenly cuts on. While it varies from mixer to mixer, the cut-on point is usually about an eighth to a quarter of the way across the crossfader. It's important to know exactly where the cut-on point is for each of the channels serviced by the crossfader.

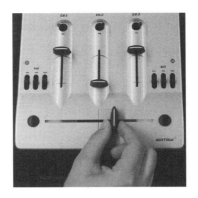

FIG. 9.2. Locating the cut-on point

To get used to finding the cut-on point:

1. Play any record on the left turntable.

2. With the right hand, move the crossfader all the way to the right, killing the sound of the record.

3. Slowly move the crossfader to the left, until you can hear the sound of the left turntable clearly. Pay attention, both visually and by feel, to the exact point where this happens. This is the cut-on point for your left turntable.

4. Practice flicking the sound of the left turntable on and off, quickly moving the crossfader back and forth over the cut-on point.

FIG. 9.3. Playing the crossfader

Repeat the steps listed, using the right turntable and your left hand to find the cut-on point for the right turntable.

Keep your movements as precise and efficient as possible. Don't go past the cut-on point any further than necessary.

Crossfader Technique

You can manipulate the crossfader simply by moving it back and forth. Or, you can play it precisely by using your fingers to attack each note, and your thumb to release them. "Think of your thumb as a spring," suggests QBert.

Here is a primer on basic crossfader technique:

1. Play any record on the left turntable.

2. Using your right hand, push the crossfader all the way over to the right with your thumb.

3. Let your thumb rest gently on the left side of the crossfader. Think of your thumb as a spring, and apply gentle pressure.

4. Allow your fingers to rear back a few inches, like a boxer winding up for a punch.

FIG. 9.4. Getting ready to strike

5. Attack the right side of the crossfader with your middle and ring fingers (or your index and middle fingers), pushing the fader over the cut-on point. Keep the pressure of your thumb constant, even though it is pushed back.

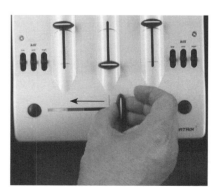

FIG. 9.5. Pushing the crossfader past the cut-on point

6. Release the pressure from your fingers, allowing your thumb to instantly push the crossfader all the way back over to the right.

FIG. 9.6. The thumb returning the crossfader to its original position

Steps 4 through 6 may be executed in a split second, depending on the length of the notes you are playing.

One-Handed Crossfader Practice

Cue up and play some white noise or a sustained tone on the left turntable. On the right turntable play a beat. Use the crossfader to play different rhythms with the noise and/or tone, like you did earlier with the up-fader and switch. Switch hands (and turntables), and do it again.

Two-Handed Scratching with the Crossfader

You can substitute the crossfader for the up-fader and switch moves already discussed. Make sure your up-fader is up and your switch is on, then use the crossfader to perform the stabs, backstabs, and cutting techniques in the last chapter.

FIG. 9.7. Scratching using the crossfader

Notice that these techniques sound slightly different when you use the crossfader. Ultimately, you want to be able to move freely between the crossfader, the switch, and the up-fader, depending on the sound you are looking for.

10.   Conclusion

I hope this has gotten you started. There's plenty more to learn, and lots of good resources out there to help.

Be patient, the more you practice, the better you'll get.

Stephen Webber

About the Author

Millions have witnessed **Stephen Webber** demonstrating turntable techniques on CNN, CBS, and NPR. His classes, books, and DVDs have been profiled in the *New York Times, Associated Press,* and *The Source* magazine. An Emmy-winning composer and a professor at Berklee College of Music, Webber has written for *Electronic Musician* and *Mix* magazine, recorded for Sony and Epic Records, and authored *Turntable Technique: The Art of the DJ,* the world's first book that teaches the turntable as a musical instrument.